Stained Glass Patterns

Color By Number
Anti Anxiety Coloring Book For Adults
For Relaxation and Meditation
Black Line Version

Thank you for your purchase!

Claim your FREE digital copy of our Highlight Reel Color By Number Book:

Check out our website: colorquestopia.com

Join our Facebook group:
facebook.com/colorquestopia

Follow us on Instagram: @colorquestopia

Did you enjoy this book?
Please leave us a review!

https://geni.us/cqreview

Our Color Palette Tips

1. **Colors corresponding to each number are shown on the back cover of the book. There are 25 colors total in this book, including one "Flesh Tone" color where you can choose any flesh tone!**

   Each number corresponds to a color shown on the back of the book. **There will sometimes be an asterisk (*) that corresponds to "Any Flesh Tone."**

   To the left of each image, there's a list of colors used within that particular image. Simply match the numbers on the images to the colors on the list. If you tear a page out of the book, you can simply use the color key on the back of the book to match your colors. If you don't have an exact color match, that's totally fine. Feel free to use a similar color or shade. Although this is a color by number book, it's completely okay to get creative and change up the colors listed. You can let your imagination run wild, and color the images with whichever colors you like and have. The numbers are here to be a guide and to allow you to color without having to focus your energy on choosing colors.

2. **If there are any spaces on an image without a number, you can go ahead and leave that space white (blank)**

   You can leave any space without a number white (blank), or you can fill that space in with any color you like. Another idea is to color that space in with a white color (for example, if you'd like to use a shiny white or a different shade of white on an image.)

3. **Bonus Images may have a slightly different color palette**

   Because the bonus images are from previous books with slightly different color palettes, they may include colors that aren't on the back of this book. Simply match them the best that you can, or choose completely different colors if you like. You are the artist and you are allowed to relax and enjoy!

Color By Number Tips

1. Relax and have fun

Let your cares slip away as you color the images. Take your time. Coloring is a meditative activity and there's no wrong way to do it. Feel free to color as you listen to music, watch TV, lounge in bed- do whatever relaxes you most! You can also color while you're out and about- on the train or at a cafe- take the book with you anywhere you go. Coloring is therapeutic and is great for stress relief and relaxation!

2. Choose your coloring tools

Everyone has their favorite coloring markers, crayons, pencils, pens- even paints! Feel free to color with any tool that you like! If you choose markers or paints, **we recommend putting a blank sheet of paper or cardboard behind each image, so that your colors don't run onto the next image.**

3. Test out your colors

Feel free to test out your colors on our Color Test Sheets at the back, and use our Custom Color Chart to make the color choices your own!

Relax and Enjoy!

1. BLACK

2. GRAY

3. DARK GRAY

4. BROWN

5. DARK BROWN

6. TAN

7. PEACH

8. RED

9. ORANGE RED

10. ORANGE

11. LIGHT YELLOW

12. YELLOW

13. GOLDEN YELLOW

14. LIGHT GREEN

15. GREEN

16. DARK GREEN

17. AQUA GREEN

18. LIGHT BLUE

19. BLUE

20. DARK BLUE

21. LILAC

22. VIOLET

23. PINK

24. VIVID PINK

4. BROWN	19. BLUE
5. DARK BROWN	20. DARK BLUE
6. TAN	21. LILAC
7. PEACH	22. VIOLET
8. RED	23. PINK
9. ORANGE RED	24. VIVID PINK
10. ORANGE	
11. LIGHT YELLOW	
12. YELLOW	
13. GOLDEN YELLOW	
14. LIGHT GREEN	
15. GREEN	
16. DARK GREEN	
17. AQUA GREEN	
18. LIGHT BLUE	

1. BLACK	16. DARK GREEN
2. GRAY	17. AQUA GREEN
3. DARK GRAY	18. LIGHT BLUE
4. BROWN	19. BLUE
5. DARK BROWN	20. DARK BLUE
6. TAN	21. LILAC
7. PEACH	22. VIOLET
8. RED	23. PINK
9. ORANGE RED	24. VIVID PINK
10. ORANGE	
11. LIGHT YELLOW	
12. YELLOW	
13. GOLDEN YELLOW	
14. LIGHT GREEN	
15. GREEN	

1. BLACK
2. GRAY
3. DARK GRAY
4. BROWN
5. DARK BROWN
6. TAN
7. PEACH
8. RED
9. ORANGE RED
10. ORANGE
11. LIGHT YELLOW
12. YELLOW
13. GOLDEN YELLOW
14. LIGHT GREEN
15. GREEN

16. DARK GREEN
17. AQUA GREEN
18. LIGHT BLUE
19. BLUE
20. DARK BLUE
21. LILAC
22. VIOLET
23. PINK
24. VIVID PINK

1. BLACK	16. DARK GREEN
2. GRAY	17. AQUA GREEN
3. DARK GRAY	18. LIGHT BLUE
4. BROWN	19. BLUE
5. DARK BROWN	20. DARK BLUE
6. TAN	21. LILAC
7. PEACH	22. VIOLET
8. RED	23. PINK
9. ORANGE RED	24. VIVID PINK
10. ORANGE	
11. LIGHT YELLOW	
12. YELLOW	
13. GOLDEN YELLOW	
14. LIGHT GREEN	
15. GREEN	

1. BLACK
2. GRAY
3. DARK GRAY
4. BROWN
5. DARK BROWN
6. TAN
7. PEACH
9. ORANGE RED
10. ORANGE
11. LIGHT YELLOW
12. YELLOW
13. GOLDEN YELLOW
14. LIGHT GREEN
15. GREEN
16. DARK GREEN

17. AQUA GREEN
18. LIGHT BLUE
19. BLUE
20. DARK BLUE
21. LILAC
22. VIOLET
23. PINK

1. BLACK	16. DARK GREEN
2. GRAY	17. AQUA GREEN
3. DARK GRAY	18. LIGHT BLUE
4. BROWN	19. BLUE
5. DARK BROWN	20. DARK BLUE
6. TAN	21. LILAC
7. PEACH	22. VIOLET
8. RED	23. PINK
9. ORANGE RED	24. VIVID PINK
10. ORANGE	
11. LIGHT YELLOW	
12. YELLOW	
13. GOLDEN YELLOW	
14. LIGHT GREEN	
15. GREEN	

1. BLACK
2. GRAY
3. DARK GRAY
4. BROWN
5. DARK BROWN
6. TAN
7. PEACH
8. RED
9. ORANGE RED
10. ORANGE
11. LIGHT YELLOW
12. YELLOW
13. GOLDEN YELLOW
18. LIGHT BLUE
19. BLUE
20. DARK BLUE
21. LILAC
22. VIOLET

1. BLACK	16. DARK GREEN
2. GRAY	17. AQUA GREEN
3. DARK GRAY	18. LIGHT BLUE
4. BROWN	19. BLUE
5. DARK BROWN	20. DARK BLUE
6. TAN	21. LILAC
7. PEACH	22. VIOLET
8. RED	23. PINK
9. ORANGE RED	24. VIVID PINK
10. ORANGE	
11. LIGHT YELLOW	
12. YELLOW	
13. GOLDEN YELLOW	
14. LIGHT GREEN	
15. GREEN	

1. BLACK
2. GRAY
3. DARK GRAY
4. BROWN
5. DARK BROWN
6. TAN
7. PEACH
8. RED
9. ORANGE RED
10. ORANGE
11. LIGHT YELLOW
12. YELLOW
13. GOLDEN YELLOW
14. LIGHT GREEN
15. GREEN
16. DARK GREEN
17. AQUA GREEN
18. LIGHT BLUE
19. BLUE
21. LILAC
23. PINK
24. VIVID PINK

4. BROWN	20. DARK BLUE
6. TAN	22. VIOLET
7. PEACH	23. PINK
8. RED	24. VIVID PINK
9. ORANGE RED	
10. ORANGE	
11. LIGHT YELLOW	
12. YELLOW	
13. GOLDEN YELLOW	
14. LIGHT GREEN	
15. GREEN	
16. DARK GREEN	
17. AQUA GREEN	
18. LIGHT BLUE	

4. BROWN

5. DARK BROWN

6. TAN

7. PEACH

8. RED

9. ORANGE RED

10. ORANGE

11. LIGHT YELLOW

12. YELLOW

13. GOLDEN YELLOW

14. LIGHT GREEN

15. GREEN

16. DARK GREEN

17. AQUA GREEN

18. LIGHT BLUE

19. BLUE

20. DARK BLUE

21. LILAC

22. VIOLET

24. VIVID PINK

1. BLACK	16. DARK GREEN
2. GRAY	17. AQUA GREEN
3. DARK GRAY	18. LIGHT BLUE
4. BROWN	19. BLUE
5. DARK BROWN	20. DARK BLUE
6. TAN	21. LILAC
7. PEACH	22. VIOLET
8. RED	23. PINK
9. ORANGE RED	24. VIVID PINK
10. ORANGE	
11. LIGHT YELLOW	
12. YELLOW	
13. GOLDEN YELLOW	
14. LIGHT GREEN	
15. GREEN	

6. TAN

7. PEACH

8. RED

9. ORANGE RED

10. ORANGE

11. LIGHT YELLOW

12. YELLOW

13. GOLDEN YELLOW

18. LIGHT BLUE

19. BLUE

20. DARK BLUE

21. LILAC

22. VIOLET

4. BROWN

5. DARK BROWN

6. TAN

7. PEACH

8. RED

9. ORANGE RED

10. ORANGE

11. LIGHT YELLOW

12. YELLOW

13. GOLDEN YELLOW

14. LIGHT GREEN

15. GREEN

16. DARK GREEN

17. AQUA GREEN

18. LIGHT BLUE

19. BLUE

20. DARK BLUE

21. LILAC

22. VIOLET

23. PINK

24. VIVID PINK

4. BROWN	19. BLUE
6. TAN	20. DARK BLUE
7. PEACH	21. LILAC
8. RED	22. VIOLET
9. ORANGE RED	23. PINK
10. ORANGE	24. VIVID PINK
11. LIGHT YELLOW	
12. YELLOW	
13. GOLDEN YELLOW	
14. LIGHT GREEN	
15. GREEN	
16. DARK GREEN	
17. AQUA GREEN	
18. LIGHT BLUE	

1. BLACK

3. DARK GRAY

4. BROWN

5. DARK BROWN

6. TAN

7. PEACH

8. RED

10. ORANGE

13. GOLDEN YELLOW

14. LIGHT GREEN

15. GREEN

16. DARK GREEN

17. AQUA GREEN

18. LIGHT BLUE

19. BLUE

20. DARK BLUE

21. LILAC

22. VIOLET

23. PINK

24. VIVID PINK

1. BLACK	18. LIGHT BLUE
2. GRAY	19. BLUE
3. DARK GRAY	20. DARK BLUE
4. BROWN	21. LILAC
5. DARK BROWN	22. VIOLET
6. TAN	23. PINK
7. PEACH	24. VIVID PINK
8. RED	
9. ORANGE RED	
10. ORANGE	
14. LIGHT GREEN	
15. GREEN	
16. DARK GREEN	
17. AQUA GREEN	

1. BLACK

2. GRAY

3. DARK GRAY

4. BROWN

5. DARK BROWN

6. TAN

7. PEACH

8. RED

9. ORANGE RED

10. ORANGE

11. LIGHT YELLOW

12. YELLOW

13. GOLDEN YELLOW

14. LIGHT GREEN

15. GREEN

16. DARK GREEN

17. AQUA GREEN

18. LIGHT BLUE

19. BLUE

20. DARK BLUE

21. LILAC

22. VIOLET

23. PINK

1. BLACK	16. DARK GREEN
2. GRAY	17. AQUA GREEN
3. DARK GRAY	18. LIGHT BLUE
4. BROWN	19. BLUE
5. DARK BROWN	20. DARK BLUE
6. TAN	21. LILAC
7. PEACH	22. VIOLET
8. RED	23. PINK
9. ORANGE RED	24. VIVID PINK
10. ORANGE	
11. LIGHT YELLOW	
12. YELLOW	
13. GOLDEN YELLOW	
14. LIGHT GREEN	
15. GREEN	

1. BLACK	16. DARK GREEN
2. GRAY	17. AQUA GREEN
3. DARK GRAY	18. LIGHT BLUE
4. BROWN	19. BLUE
5. DARK BROWN	20. DARK BLUE
6. TAN	21. LILAC
7. PEACH	22. VIOLET
8. RED	23. PINK
9. ORANGE RED	24. VIVID PINK
10. ORANGE	
11. LIGHT YELLOW	
12. YELLOW	
13. GOLDEN YELLOW	
14. LIGHT GREEN	
15. GREEN	

ENJOY BONUS IMAGES FROM SOME OF OUR OTHER FUN COLOR BY NUMBER BOOKS!

FIND ALL OF OUR BOOKS ON AMAZON

Dazzling Patterns
Color By Number
Black Background
Anti Anxiety Coloring Book For Adults

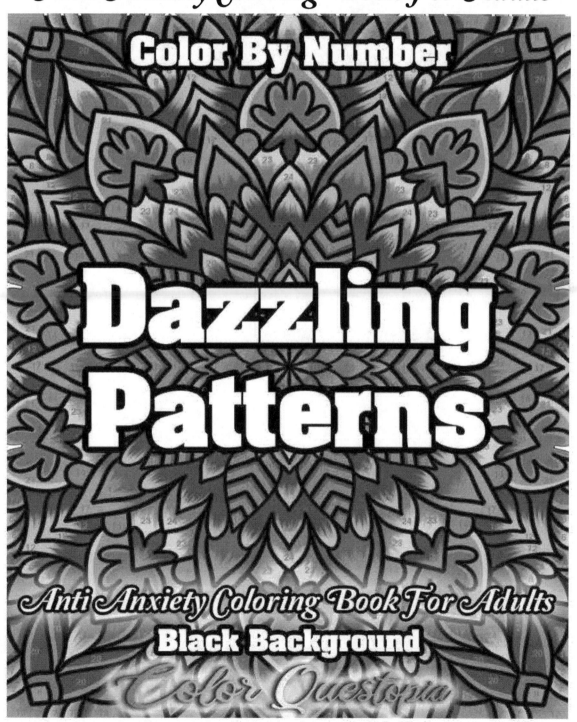

6. Tan

8. Red

10. Orange

12. Yellow

14. Light Green

15. Green

16. Dark Green

17. Aqua Green

18. Light Blue

20. Dark Blue

21. Lilac

22. Violet

23. Pink

24. Vivid Pink

STAINED GLASS
BLACK BACKGROUND
Color By Number For Adults

4.   Brown

10.   Orange

15.   Green

16.   Dark Green

17.   Aqua Green

18.   Light Blue

20.   Dark Blue

Relaxation
Black Background
Color By Number
Coloring Book for Adults

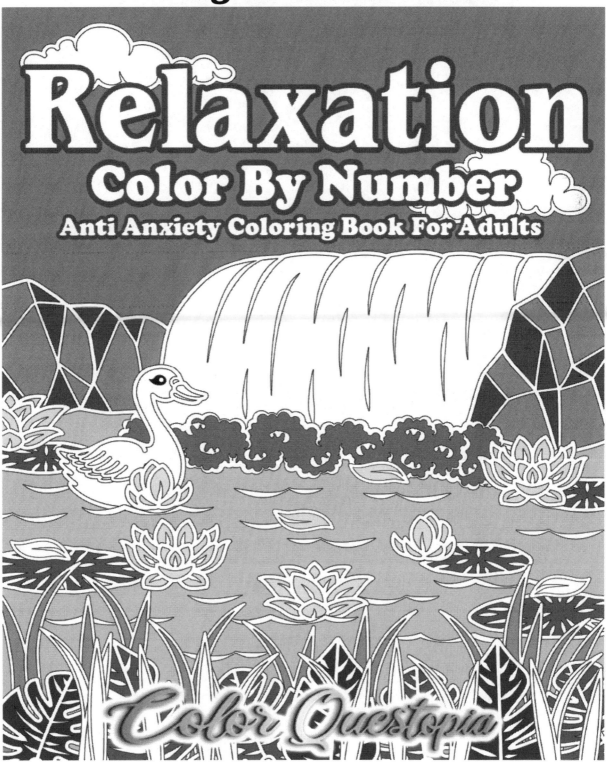

* Any Flesh Tone   18. Light Blue

3. Dark Gray   19. Blue

5. Dark Brown   20. Dark Blue

6. Tan   21. Lilac

9. Orange Red   22. Violet

10. Orange

12. Yellow

13. Golden Yellow

14. Light Green

15. Green

16. Dark Green

Halloween Patterns
Color By Number
Coloring Book for Adults
Black Background

Halloween
Patterns

Color By Number Coloring For Adults

Black Background

Color Questopia

1. Black

4. Brown

7. Peach

8. Red

10. Orange

12. Yellow

15. Green

17. Aqua Green

19. Blue

21. Lilac

22. Violet

Autumn Patterns
BLACK BACKGROUND
Color By Number
Coloring Book for Adults

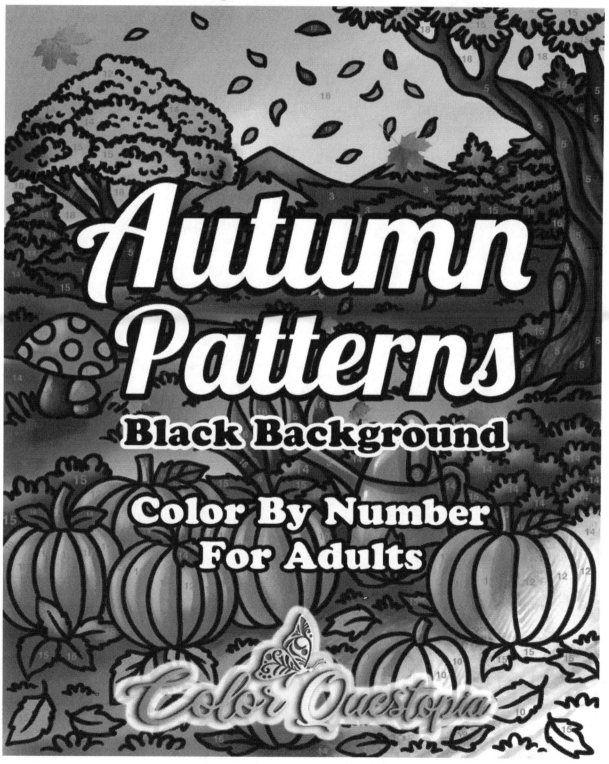

2. Gray

4. Brown

5. Dark Brown

6. Tan

7. Peach

8. Red

10. Orange

12. Yellow

14. Light Green

15. Green

16. Dark Green

19. Blue

22. Violet

24. Vivid Pink

Custom Color Chart

Medium: _ _ _ _ _ _ _ _ _

Brand: _ _ _ _ _ _ _ _ _

1. Black _____

2. Gray _____

3. Dark Gray _____

4. Brown _____

5. Dark Brown _____

6. Tan _____

7. Peach _____

8. Red _____

9. Orange Red _____

10. Orange _____

11. Light Yellow _____

12. Yellow _____

13. Golden Yellow _____

14. Light Green _____

15. Green _____

16. Dark Green _____

17. Aqua Green _____

18. Light Blue _____

19. Blue _____

20. Dark Blue _____

21. Lilac _____

22. Violet _____

23. Pink _____

24. Vivid Pink _____

* Flesh Tone _____

Custom Color Chart

Medium: _ _ _ _ _ _ _ _ _   Brand: _ _ _ _ _ _ _ _ _

1. _____

2. _____

3. _____

4. _____

5. _____

6. _____

7. _____

8. _____

9. _____

10. _____

11. _____

* 12. _____

13. _____

14. _____

15. _____

16. _____

17. _____

18. _____

19. _____

20. _____

21. _____

22. _____

23. _____

24. _____

* _____

Color Testing Sheet

Color Testing Sheet

Made in the USA
Columbia, SC
08 January 2025

51398284R00050